**Stickers for 'Shark Sudoku' on Page 2**

**Stickers for 'Snappy Order' on Page 7**

Sticker for 'Stick-a-Shark' on Page 3

Sticker for 'Stick-a-Shark' on Page 3

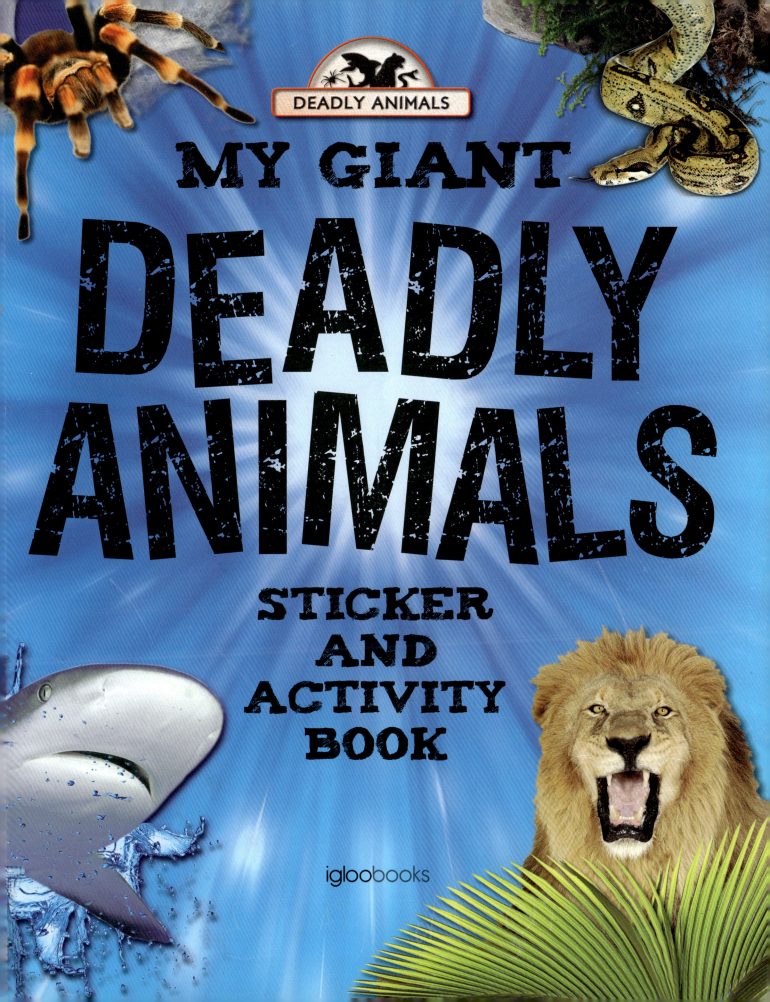

# MY GIANT
# DEADLY
# ANIMALS

## STICKER
## AND
## ACTIVITY
## BOOK

igloobooks

# Shark Sudoku

This grid shows pictures of four sharks. Each shark should appear once in each row and each column. Find the stickers on your sticker sheet to complete the grid.

# Shadow Match

Can you match the shadows to each of the sharks? Which shadow is the odd one out?

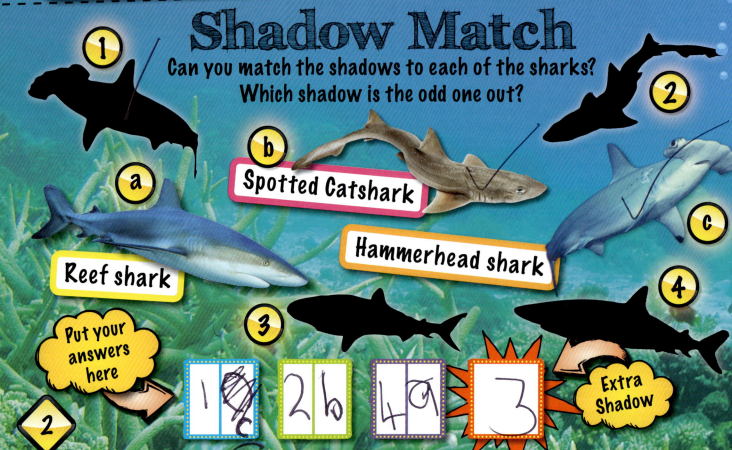

Spotted Catshark

Hammerhead shark

Reef shark

Put your answers here

1c    2b    4a    3

Extra Shadow

# Stick-a-Shark

Can you find the sticker tiles on your sticker sheet
to complete this shark picture?

Find the answers on
page 46, 47 and 48

**Who Am I Clue!**
The Hammerhead shark
is named for its flat,
hammer-shaped head.

3

# Cool Camouflage

Some sharks have amazing camouflage, so they can blend into their surroundings. Can you match each of these descriptions to the sharks pictured below.

a

3 "My skin has a striped pattern, like rippled waves."

c

**Blue shark**

b

**Great White shark**

1 "The skin on my back is yellow and speckled, so I look sandy."

**Lemon shark**

2 "My skin is the color of the wide open ocean that I swim in."

e

4 "I have a white underbelly and a dark gray back, so I'm hard to spot from above or below."

d

5 "My flat body helps me blend into the sea floor."

**Angel shark**

**Tiger shark**

Put your answers here

| e | 5 | c | 4 | b | 1 | d | 3 | a | 2 |

# Shark Shadow Code

Can you crack the code and work out the name of the shark?

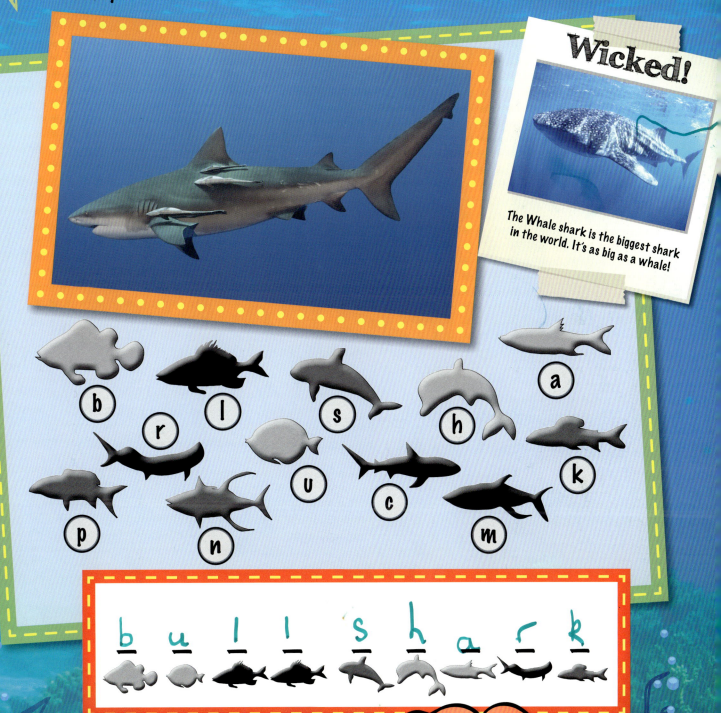

## Wicked!

The Whale shark is the biggest shark in the world. It's as big as a whale!

b    r    l    s    h    a

p    n    u    c    m    k

**b u l l   s h a r k**

Find the answers on page 46, 47 and 48

## Who Am I Clue!

The Whale shark has a bright spotted pattern on its back, that looks like stars in the sky.

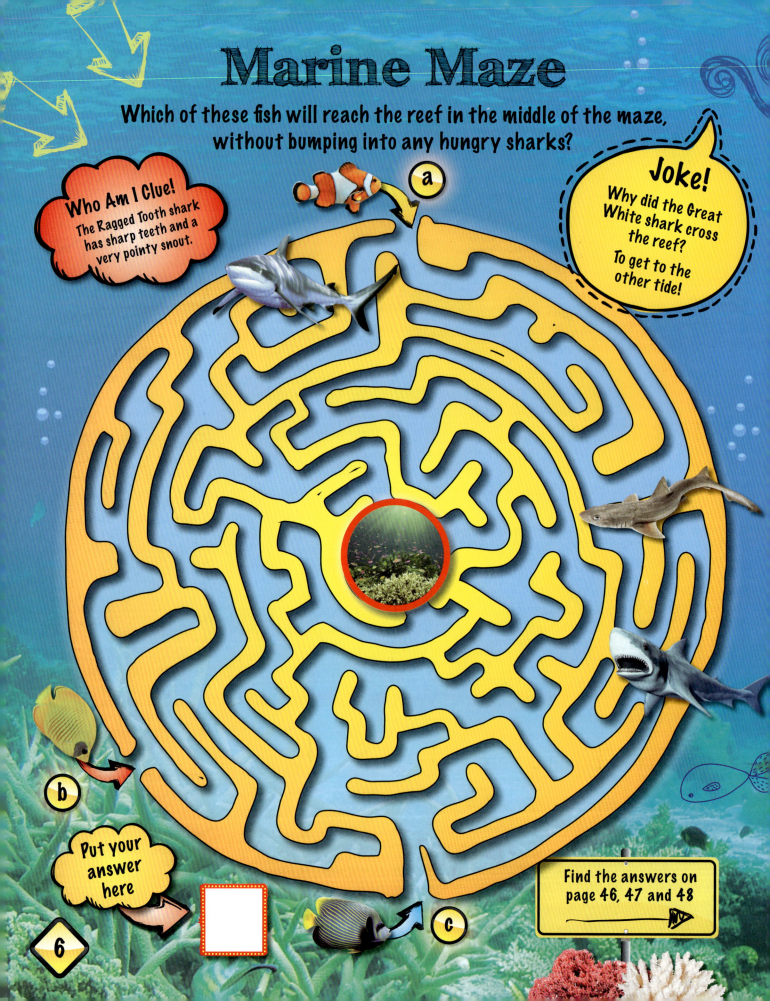

# Snappy Order

Can you work out what comes next in these shark tooth sequences?
Use the stickers on your sticker sheet to complete each line.

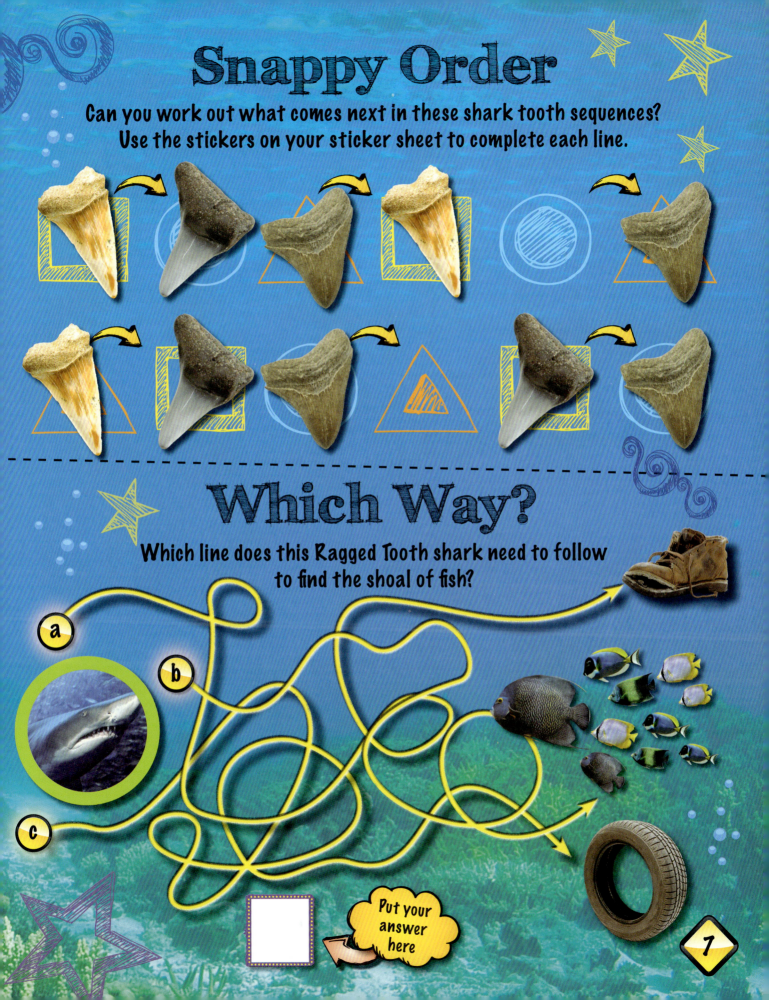

# Which Way?

Which line does this Ragged Tooth shark need to follow
to find the shoal of fish?

a

b

c

Put your
answer
here

# Under the Sea

Race across the sea to the finish line.

## HOW TO PLAY:

1. Each player choose a sticker from the sticker sheet and stick it to a coin. Place your coin counters on the START space.

2. Take turns to roll the dice and move your counter, following the instructions on the spaces you land on.

3. The first player to reach the FINISH space wins!

## WHAT YOU NEED:

2-4 Players

A dice

Coins for counters

**START**

1

**2** Chase a shoal of fish. Move forward TWO spaces.

3

**14** FACT! A shark may have over 20,000 teeth in its lifetime.

13

**15** Stop to explore a sunken ship. MISS a turn.

16

**17** FACT! Sharks don't have bones, they have cartilage.

**18** Find a tasty lunch. Move forward TWO spaces.

19

**20** FACT! The Goblin shark is so rare, very few humans have ever seen it. It is bright pink and has a very sharp, long nose.

8

Sticker for 'Stick-a-Shark' on Page 3

Sticker for 'Stick-a-Shark' on Page 3

Stickers for 'Complete the Creature' on Page 11

# Complete the Creature

Find the missing stickers on your sticker
sheet to complete this shark.

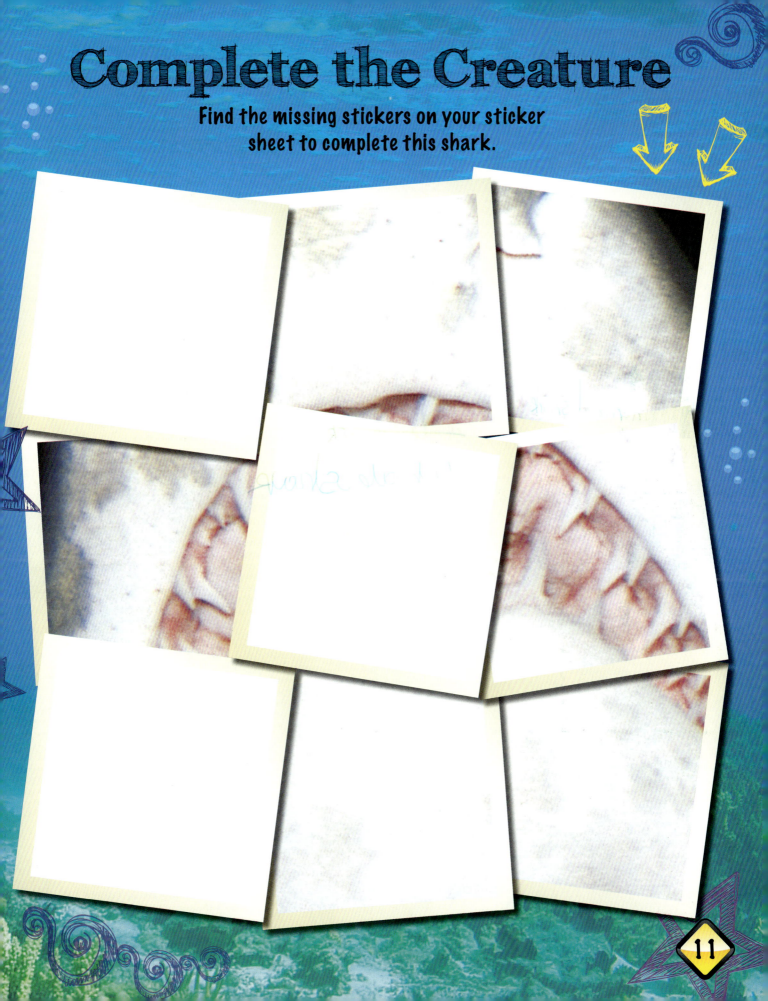

# A Pair of Predators

Can you match each pair of sharks?
Which one does not have a pair?

## Wow!

Sharks live in every ocean in the world.

**a**

**e**

**d**

**c**

### Joke!
What kind of sharks would you find in heaven?
Angel sharks.

**1**

**2**

**3**

**4**

**b**

Extra Shark

Put your answers here

Find the answers on page 46, 47 and 48

12

# Ferocious Facts

Can you work out which of the below statements are true and which are false?

Put your answers in the white boxes

**a** "Sharks have over one hundred bones in their bodies."

**b** "Most sharks have four rows of teeth."

**c** "Some sharks can launch their whole bodies out of the water."

**d** "Sharks can smell one drop of blood in a million drops of water."

**e** "Sharks have really bad senses."

**f** "Sharks are fish."

**g** "There is a type of shark that is bubblegum pink."

# Ship Shape

Join the dots to see what the shark is swimming towards.

## Awesome!

All sharks have an extra sense which enables them to detect the movement of other living animals in the water.

13

# Who Am I?

Can you work out the names of the sharks in these pictures?
Look back through the pages of this book to find clues that will help you.

**a** hammerhead shark

**b** Whale-Shark

whale shark

**c**

# Deadly Animal Difference

Take a look at these two pictures. Can you spot six differences?
Circle the differences you find in box b.

**a**

**b**

# Colorful Coral

Use your stickers to decorate this coral reef.
What kind of shark is already swimming in the picture?

_ _ M _ _ R H _ A _

Put your answer here

## Wicked!

Sharks are a kind of fish. Some even hang out in shoals.

## Joke!
What kind of sandwiches do sharks like best?
Peanut butter and jellyfish!

Find the answers on page 46, 47 and 48

15

# Spider Squares

Copy this super cool, creepy spider into the grid square-by-square.

## Wicked!

The Black Widow female spider is twice as big as the male. Her egg sac is huge and can contain up to 400 eggs!

# Spider Sticker Match

Can you work out which stickers from your sticker sheet match the spider names below?

Goliath
Bird-eating spider

Cobalt Blue
tarantula

Wasp spider

Palm spider

**Joke!**
What do spiders eat in Paris? French flies!

# Which Way?

Which thread should this Black Widow spider follow to get to the delicious dinner that's caught in her web?

a

b

c

Put your answer here

Find the answers on page 46, 47 and 48

17

# Super Spider Zoom

Can you work out which two of these close-up pictures come from each creepy spider?

a

b

c

d

e

f

1

2

3

Put your answers here

e
c
l

a
f
2

b
d
3

18

# Letter Web

Unscramble the letters to find out what type of spider made this web.

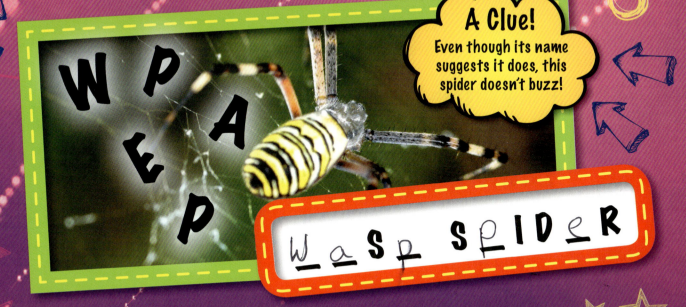

**A Clue!**
Even though its name suggests it does, this spider doesn't buzz!

W P A E P

W a s p   S p i d e r

---

# Let's Draw!

This spider should have eight legs. Finish drawing the missing legs of the spider, then use your best pens and pencils to color it in.

**Cool!**
Some species of Orb spider create a zig-zag pattern on their web to attract prey and make the web stronger.

Find the answers on page 46, 47 and 48

19

# How Much Do You Know?

Can you work out which spider matches
each description below?

1. My bite can be deadly and I have a red hourglass shape on my abdomen. →  b

2. Lots of people keep me as a pet. →  d

3. I make my web in the shape of a funnel and my fangs can grow really long. →  a

4. I can eat larger animals, such as lizards, birds and frogs. →  c

a  Funnel-web spider

b  Black Widow spider

c  Bird-eating tarantula

d  Tarantula

# Spidery Spot

Can you spot the four differences between these two spiders?

a

b

**JOKE!**

What did one spider say to the other?

"Time's fun when you're having flies!"

Find the answers on page 46, 47 and 48

21

# Spider Sudoku

This grid shows lots of things that spiders like to eat.
Each picture appears once in each column and each row.
Find the missing pictures on your sticker sheet to complete the grid.

Find the answers on
page 46, 47 and 48

# Catch the Critters

There are lots of crawly critters in this creepy picture.
Can you count them all?

**Crab spider**

**Trapdoor spider**

**Jumping spider**

**Tarantula spider**

# Awesome!

Spider silk is five times stronger than steel of the same diameter.

# Cobwebs and Venom

Test your skills in this Cobwebs and Venom game.

WHAT YOU NEED:

**2-4 Players**

**A dice**

**Coins for counters**

FACT!
There are over 40,000 different species of spider!

41. 42. 43. 44. 45.
40. 38. 37. 36.
39.
21. 22. 23. 24. 25.
20. 18. 17. 16.
19.
1. START 2. 3. 4. 5.

1. Choose stickers from your sticker sheet and stick them to your coins to use as a counters. Place the counters on the START square.

2. Take turns to roll the dice and move your counter. If you land on a cobweb you can climb up, but if you land on venom, you have to slide down!

3. The first player to reach the FINISH square wins.

**Joke!**
Why do spiders spin webs? Because they can't knit!

FINISH

**FACT!**
The largest tarantulas can be the size of a dinner plate!

**FACT!**
The Raft spider can skate across water!

**FACT!**
Spiders are found on every continent in the world except Antarctica!

# Creepy Crawly Quiz

Can you work out which of these super spider facts are true and which are false?

Write T or F in the white boxes when you think you know.

1. All spiders have eight legs.
2. All spiders spin webs.
3. Some spiders can change colour.
4. Male spiders are usually bigger than the females.

T F F
T
F

# Spidery Shadows

Can you work out which shadow below comes from this creepy spider?

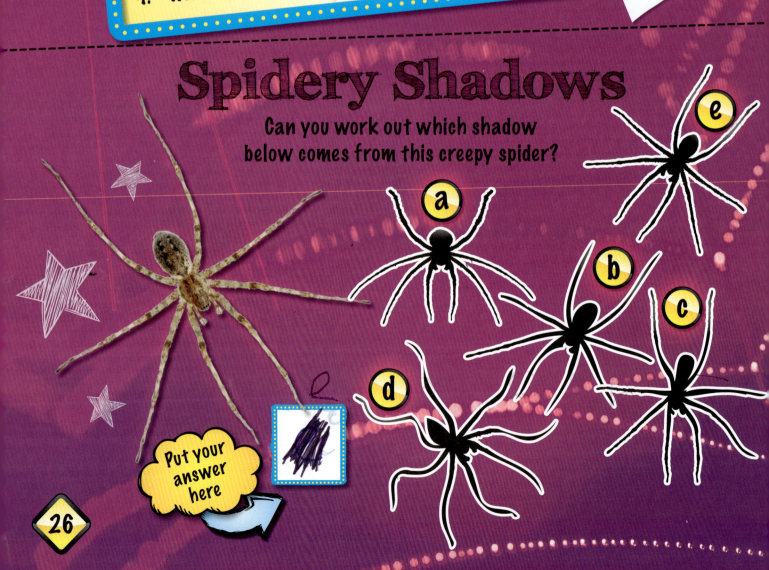

a
b
c
d
e

Put your answer here

# Maze Madness

Can you work out which fly will find its way safely to the middle of the maze, without getting eaten by any lurking spiders?

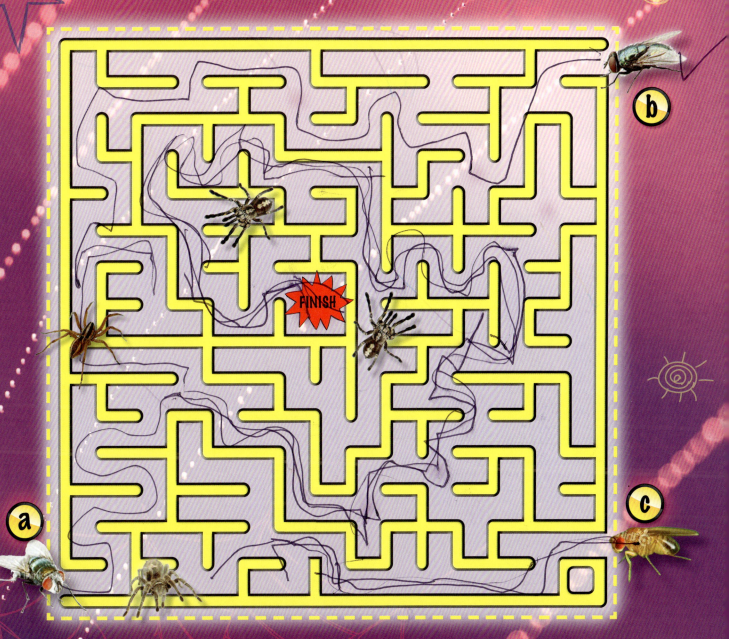

**Joke!**

Why did the spider buy a computer?

She wanted a website!

Find the answers on page 46, 47 and 48

Put your answer here

# Scrambled Spiders

These spiders are all mixed up.
Can you match up each of the spider halves?

**Wow!**

Instead of building a web, the Wolf spider hunts and chases insects to catch them. Just like a real wolf!

1

2

3

4

5

a

b

c

d

e

Put your answers here

| 1 | d |
|---|---|

| 3 | ℮ |
|---|---|

| 2 | a |
|---|---|

| 4 | ℮ |
|---|---|

| 5 | b |
|---|---|

Find the answers on page 46, 47 and 48

# Remember Me

Study these spiders for thirty seconds, then cover up the pictures and see how many names you can remember.

**1** Brown Recluse

**2** Black Widow

**3** Australian Funnel-Web spider

**Wicked!**

Some spiders, like the Crab spider, can change color to blend into their surroundings.

**4** Redback spider

**5** Wolf spider

**6** Sac spider

**7** Jumping spider

**8** Baboon spider

1.

2.

3.

4.

5.

6.

7.

8.

9.

10.

Put your answers here

# Reptile Race

### Slither to the finishing line in this exciting reptile race.

## HOW TO PLAY:

1. Each player must choose a sticker from the sticker sheet and stick it to a coin to use as a counter. Place the coins on the START space.

2. Take turns to roll the dice and follow the instructions on the spaces you land on.

3. The first player to the reach the FINISH space wins.

## WHAT YOU NEED:

**A dice**

**Coins for counters**

**2-4 Players**

**1.**

**START**

**2.**

**FACT!** Snakes use their forked tongues to smell as well as taste.

**3.**

**4.** Take a nap in a nearby tree. MISS a turn.

**5.**

**6.**

**7.** Go for a swim in a river. Move forward THREE spaces.

**8.**

**9.**

# Forget Me Not

Study these big cats for thirty seconds, then cover up the pictures and see how many names you can remember. Write them in the white box below.

1
White Tiger

2
Cougar

3
Leopard

4
Black Panther

5
Cheetah

6
Tiger

7
Lion

8
Lynx

**Cub Clue!**
Male lion cubs don't grow a mane until they are almost two.

1.
2.
3.
4.
5.
6.
7.
8.

Put your answers here

Find the answers on page 46, 47 and 48

# Safari Spot

The speech bubbles below describe big cats that have been spotted in the wild. Can you find the stickers on your sticker sheet that match each description?

**1** "On the savanna, I saw cats running faster than any animal on earth."

**2** "On safari, I saw a pride of cats relaxing."

**3** "In the jungle, I saw a spotted cat taking a nap in a tree."

**4** "Hiking in the mountains, I saw a big cat hunting."

**5** "Walking through the jungle, I passed a stripy big cat."

**Joke!**
Who helped the old lion cross the street?
A cub scout!

**Wicked!**

Lions greet each other by rubbing heads, or licking.

# Paw Print Path

Which line should the cub follow to find his mother?

a

b

c

# Letter Scramble

Can you unscramble these names and
fill in the answer boxes?

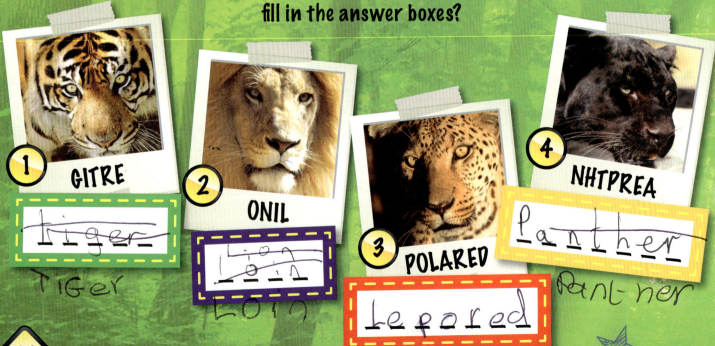

1 GITRE

Tiger

Tiger

2 ONIL

Lion

Lion

3 POLARED

lepored

4 NHTPREA

Panther

Pant-ner

# Who's Missing?

Can you circle the two big cats that are in picture a, but not in picture b?
There is also an extra cat in picture b, can you circle it?

**Cub Clue!**
Baby bobcats already have their spotty fur and pointy ears when they are born.

Find the answers on page 46, 47 and 48

35

# Heads and Tails

Can you match the correct head to the correct tail?
Write the pairs in the boxes below.

QUIZ!

One of these cats is not a big cat, but a regular house cat. Can you work out which one?

Put your answers here

a 2 | d 1 | e 4 | c 5 | b 3

Find the answers on page 46, 47 and 48

# Big Cat Habitat

Can you match each of these cats to their correct habitat?
Write your answers in the boxes down the middle of the puzzle.

**1**

**CLUE!**
"Siberian tigers can endure very cold temperatures."

| c | 1 |
|---|---|

**a**

**2**

**CLUE!**
"Cheetahs need lots of open space to run."

| a | 2 |
|---|---|

**CLUE!**
Two of these cats come from the same habitat, can you work out which ones?

**b**

**3**

**CLUE!**
"Lions like to rest in open grassland.

**c**

**4**

**CLUE!**
"Panthers like to climb trees in the jungle."

| b | 3 |
|---|---|

| b | 4 |
|---|---|

**d**

**5**

**CLUE!**
Cougars are also called "Mountain lions."

| d | 5 |
|---|---|

# Savanna Scene

Find some stickers on your sticker sheet to decorate this African savanna scene.

## Awesome!

Some scientists believe Clouded leopards may be related to ancient saber-toothed cats.

**Cub Clue!**
When leopards are cubs their fur is so thick, you can hardly see their spots.

# Furry Friends

The patterns below belong to all different kinds of animals.
Can you circle the patterns that belong to big cats?

Cheater

gir graffe

elfant

Zebra

Lepord

Tiger

Find the answers on
page 46, 47 and 48

39

Stickers for
'Jigsaw Roar' on Page 45

Sticker for
'Toothless Tiger' on Page 46

Stickers for
'Find the Friends' on Page 44

Stickers for 'Safari Spot' on Page 33

# Big Cat Hunt

Can you find all of the big cats hiding in this picture?

Cool!

Lions have the loudest roar of any big cat.

Panther — 4

Lion — 1

Tiger — 4

Cheetah — 3

# Cub Clues

Each of these cubs is going to grow up to be a big cat.
Can you work out what kind of cat each of these cubs will be?

**CLUE!**

Look through this book to find clues that will help you work it out.

1

Panther

2

_ _ _ _ _ _

3

_ _ _ _ _ _ _

4

white tiger

5

Lion

Find the answers on page 46, 47 and 48

43

# Find the Friends

Each of these cats is missing their friend. Find a friend for each one on your sticker sheets to complete the pairs.

### Cub Clue!
White tiger cubs keep the blue eyes and pink noses they are born with.

# Jigsaw Roar

Can you find the missing pieces on your sticker sheet to finish this picture?

**Cool!**

Every tiger has a different stripe pattern on their coat.

**JOKE!**
What's the difference between a tiger and a lion?
The tiger has the mane part missing!

Find the answers on page 46, 47 and 48

# Toothless Tiger

This tiger is missing something! Find the missing sticker on your sticker sheet and complete the picture so he can eat his lunch.

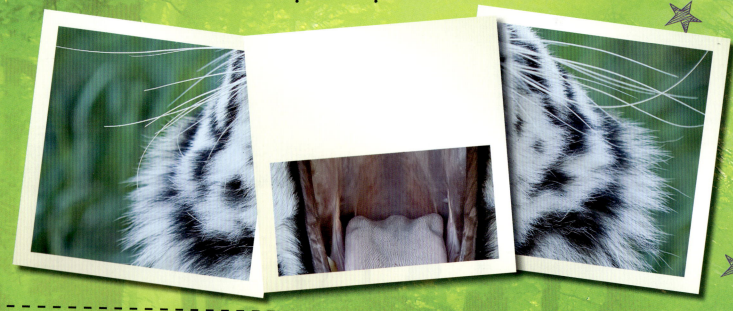

# Answers

## Page 2
### Shark Sudoku

1.

2.

3.

4.

### Shadow Match

1 - c     2 - b     3 is the extra shadow
4 - a

## Page 4
### Cool Camouflage

1 - b     2 - a     3 - d     4 - c     5 - e

## Page 5
### Shark Shadow Code

The correct answer is Bull shark

## Page 6
### Marine Maze

The correct answer is fish a

## Page 7
### Snappy Order

### Which Way

Correct answer is line b

## Page 10
### Shark Spotting

1 - c     2 - d     3 - a     4 - b

## Page 12
### A Pair of Predators

1 - b     2 - a     3 - e     4 - d
The extra shark is c

# Answers

## Page 13
### Ferocious Facts

a - False    b - True    c - True    d - True

e - False    f - True    g - True

## Page 14
### Who Am I?

a - Hammerhead shark    b - Whale shark

c - Ragged Tooth shark

### Deadly Animal Difference

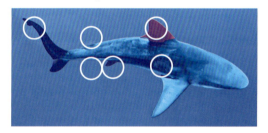

## Page 15
### Colorful Coral

The answer is Hammerhead

## Page 17
### Spider Sticker Match

Goliath Bird-eating spider    Cobalt Blue tarantula    Wasp spider    Palm spider

### Which Way

The spider should follow thread b

## Page 18
### Super Spider Zoom

1 - c, e    2 - a, f    3 - b, d

## Page 19
### Letter Web

The answer is Wasp spider

## Page 20
### How Much Do You Know?

1 - b    2 - d    3 - a    4 - c

## Page 21
### Spidery Spot

## Page 22
### Spider Sudoku

1    2    3    4

## Page 23
### Catch the Critters

Crab spiders - 6    Jumping spiders - 7

Trapdoor spiders - 4    Tarantulas - 3

## Page 26
### Creepy Crawly Quiz

1 - True    2 - False    3 - True    4 - False

### Spidery Shadows

The matching shadow is e

## Page 27
### Maze Madness

The correct answer is a

## Page 28
### Scrambled Spiders

1 - d    2 - a    3 - c    4 - e    5 - b

# Answers

## Page 33
### Safari Spot

1.

2.

3.

4.

5.

## Page 34
### Paw Print Path

Correct answer is line b

### Letter Scramble
1 - Tiger     3 - Leopard
2 - Lion     4 - Panther

## Page 35
### Who's Missing?

Picture a

Picture b

## Page 36
### Heads and Tails

1 - d     2 - a     3 - b     4 - e     5 - c

2 - a is a house cat

## Page 37
### Big Cat Habitat

1 - c     2 - a     3 - a     4 - b     5 - d

## Page 39
### Furry Friends

Tiger

Cheetah

Leopard

## Page 42
### Big Cat Hunt

Panthers - 4     Tigers - 4
Lion - 1     Cheetahs - 3

## Page 43
### Cub Clues

1 - Panther     4 - White tiger
2 - Bobcat     5 - Lion
3 - Leopard